Disclaimer:

The Author, Brian Ernest Hayward, is not a legal, financial, or medical professional, and the content provided is for informational purposes only. Always consult with a qualified professional for advice in these areas, as
Brian Ernest Hayward is not responsible for any actions taken based on this information."

Copyright © 2024 by Brian Ernest Hayward and Published by Brian Hayward for Hayward House Publishing Published by Hayward House and Big Book Box A Member of the Brian Hayward Group All rights reserved. No part of this publication may be reproduced, stored in a retrieval system, or transmitted, in any form or by any means, electronic, mechanical, photocopying, recording, or otherwise, without the prior written permission of the publisher. For information and inquiries , address Hayward House publishing and Hayward Press, Savannah, Ga 31405, Library of Congress Cataloging-in-Publication Data. Hayward, Brian. TITLE=In Jesus Mighty Name Series, Journal WRITING for success in your life / Brian Hayward. p. cm.

PAPER BACK EDITION
ISBN: 9798334055674
Imprint: Independently published

Self-control. 2. Self-management (Psychology) 3. Success. 4. Success in business. 31405, or visit us at
https://www.amazon.com/Brian-Ernest-Hayward/e/B06XT464NM

PRAYER FOR MYSELF AND MY READERS

I was taught by my teacher, Pastor Bill Winston, this prayer. This prayer has served me well, and in due time it will serve you well. Father I come before you in Jesus name, thank you for the anointing that's on me and these lips of clay. I know that because of your blessing, I speak this word today with excellency, accuracy, and boldness. I thank you for thinking through my mind and speaking through my lips and this word will come forth unhindered, and unchecked by any outside force. Now I give you the praise for it and I fully expect signs, wonders, and miracles to confirm your word preached in Jesus name,

AUTHOR BIOGRAPHY

Brian Ernest Hayward is a passionate Author and Inspirational Speaker, internationally known for his unwavering dedication to creating positive change through the power of words. From religious and success books, to adult coloring books and artist BUSINESS, HOW-TO BOOKS, his writings touch on over 400 different subjects. Today, all of Brian's publications are sold worldwide across multiple formats (Paperback, Kindle, and Large Print) and are translated into 21 different languages. He has also participated in over 100 speaking engagements spanning over 38 states.

Table Of Contents

Introduction: Innovate & Accelerate: Boost Your Ideas! ... 6

Chapter 1: Embracing Continuous Improvement ... 18

Chapter 2: Assessing Your Current Innovations ... 28

Chapter 3: Developing an Improvement Plan ... 36

Chapter 4: Implementing Feedback and Iteration ... 45

Chapter 5: Building and Sustaining Momentum ... 53

Chapter 6: Overcoming Obstacles and Challenges. ... 61

Chapter 7: Using Technology and Tools ... 68

Chapter 8: Building a Culture of Continuous Improvement	74
Chapter 9: Measuring and Communicating Results	82
Chapter 10: The Power of Persistent Improvement	88
Chapter 11: Practical Solutions for Ongoing Improvement	97
Chapter 12: Keeping Motivation and Commitment to Excellence	109
Conclusion – The Power of Persistent Improvement	117
Bibliography	130
NOTES	131

Introduction: Innovate & Accelerate: Boost Your Ideas!

Welcome to "How to Get on with Improving Your Other Innovations: And Build Momentum." Authoring this book has been an exhilarating journey spanning three months, each filled with challenges, breakthroughs, and late-night writing sessions. This manual is designed to guide the ever-evolving landscape of innovation, providing practical strategies, real-world examples, and a dash of humor to make the journey enjoyable.

In the first month, the foundation was laid. This was the research phase, where I delved into countless articles, case studies, and success stories from various industries. The goal was to gather a wealth of knowledge on continuous improvement and momentum building. This period was about planting seeds and nurturing ideas that would eventually blossom into the comprehensive guide you now hold.

The second month was dedicated to development. With a solid outline in place, I began fleshing out each chapter, weaving in practical advice, and adding real-world examples to illustrate key points. This phase  was marked by a flurry of creativity, with ideas flowing freely and words coming together to form coherent, engaging content. Revisions were a constant companion, ensuring that each chapter was polished and precise.

The final month was the refinement phase. This involved gathering feedback from early readers, incorporating their suggestions, and fine-tuning the content to ensure clarity and impact. It was a time of iteration, much like the principles outlined in this book. Each chapter was revisited and revised, ensuring that the final product was as informative and engaging as possible.

So, why is this book important? "In a world that's constantly evolving, staying stagnant is not an option." Innovations, no matter how groundbreaking, need continuous refinement to remain relevant and effective. This book emphasizes the importance of never settling for "good enough" and striving for excellence through persistent effort and improvement. By continuously improving your innovations, you not only stay ahead of the competition but also unlock new levels of success and satisfaction.

What exactly will you learn from this book? The focus is on building momentum and achieving tangible results through continuous improvement. Each chapter provides a step-by-step guide to enhance your projects, from forming your current innovations to developing detailed improvement plans, gathering feedback, and using technology. Each aim is to equip you with the tools and strategies to turn your ideas into impactful realities.

Timing is crucial in the world of innovation. The best time to start improving your innovations is now. This book will guide you on how to prioritize tasks, manage actively, and create a road to success. Whether you are at the beginning of your innovation journey or looking to enhance an established project, the principles outlined here are timeless and universally applicable.

The concepts in this book are designed for global application. Innovation knows no boundaries, and the need for continuous improvement is universal. Whether you're a styling city or a quiet village, the strategies in this book can help you drive positive change and build momentum. The principles apply across industries and regions, providing a global roadmap to success.

How do you implement these concepts? This book is packed with practical steps  that will make the implementation process straightforward and manageable. From setting realistic goals to using the latest tech tools, each chapter breaks down complex concepts into actionable advice. By the end of this book, you'll have a clear, practical plan to improve your innovations and build unstoppable momentum.

The journey starts with an assessment of your current innovations. You'll learn to evaluate your projects, name strengths and weaknesses, and set achievable improvement goals. This foundational step is crucial for understanding where you stand and what needs to be done to move forward.

The next step is to develop a structured improvement plan. This involves outlining the steps needed to achieve your goals, defining milestones, and setting timelines. A well-thought-out plan provides a clear path to ensuring you stay on track and make consistent progress.

Gathering feedback and iterating on your improvements is an ongoing process. You'll learn how to collect valuable insights from users, stakeholders, and team members and use this feedback to refine your innovations. This iterative approach ensures that your projects continue to evolve and improve over time.

Building and sustaining momentum is crucial for long-term success. You'll discover strategies to keep progress, celebrate small wins, and avoid stagnation. Momentum is the driving force that propels your projects forward, and this book provides the tools to keep it going strong.

Overcoming obstacles is an inevitable part of any improvement journey. This  book will equip you with practical solutions for tackling common challenges, emphasizing resilience and persistence by addressing your difficulties and keeping your head-on projects on track.

Leveraging it by addressing obstacles head-on technology and tools is essential in today's digital age. From automation to data analytics, you'll learn how to use modern tools to enhance your improvement efforts. Technology can streamline tasks, offer valuable insights, and significantly boost efficiency.

Building a culture of continuous improvement within your team or organization is vital. This involves fostering a growth mindset, promoting collaboration, and investing in training and development. A strong culture of continuous improvement ensures that everyone is aligned and motivated to contribute to the process.

Measuring and communicating results is the final piece of the puzzle. Key Performance Indicators (KPIs) help track progress and evaluate the effectiveness of your efforts. Effective communication ensures that stakeholders are informed and engaged, providing transparency and fostering support.

As you read this book, you'll meet inspiring case studies of companies and individuals who have successfully embraced continuous improvement. These real-world examples illustrate the principles in action, providing practical insights and inspiration for your improvement journey.

By the end of this book, you'll have a solid foundation and a comprehensive toolkit for continuous improvement. The real work begins after you close the book. It's about applying what you've learned, staying committed to the process, and never settling for mediocrity. Continuous improvement is a marathon, not a sprint; each brings you closer to excellence.

So, whether you want to enhance an existing innovation or embark on a new project, this book is your guide to achieving excellence. With a blend of practical advice, real-world examples, and a touch of humor, we'll make the journey of continuous improvement enjoyable and rewarding. Embrace the process, stay curious, and prepare to advance your innovations.

Welcome to the exciting world of continuous improvement. Let's embark on this adventure together, one step at a time. By the end of this journey, you'll improve your innovations and develop a mindset of perpetual growth and excellence. Here's to continuous improvement, relentless momentum, and a future of innovation and success.

Chapter 1: Embracing Continuous Improvement

Let's kick things off with a story. Imagine a world-renowned chef who perfected a recipe for the most delicious soup. His restaurant thrived, and people came far and wide for a taste. However, as time passed, the chef noticed fewer returning customers. His soup, though still delicious, had lost its novelty. Instead of resting on his laurels, he began experimenting, adding new ingredients, and enhancing the flavors. His relentless pursuit of improvement brought a return and even earned him a Michelin star. This is the power of continuous improvement.

Why is continuous improvement crucial? Think about your smartphone. Every year, there's a new model with better features, improved performance, and enhanced design. If companies stopped at the first successful version, they would quickly fall behind in the fast-paced tech world. Continuous improvement keeps products relevant, competitive, and valuable to customers. It's about staying ahead of the curve and constantly pushing the boundaries of what's possible.

In this book, we'll explore how you can apply the principles of continuous improvement to your innovations. Whether you're an entrepreneur, a team leader, or a creative individual, there's always room to enhance your projects. Continuous improvement isn't about making radical changes but minor, incremental adjustments that add up over time. Like sharpening a knife, each improvement makes your innovation more practical.

The beauty of continuous improvement is that it's a journey, not a destination. It's an ongoing process that requires dedication, curiosity, and a willingness to learn. No matter how successful your innovation is today, there's always potential for it to be even better tomorrow. This mindset of perpetual growth sets apart the good from the great and the ordinary from the extraordinary.

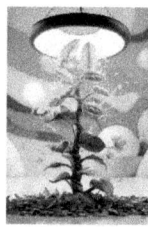 Let's face it; change can be intimidating. But with the right approach, it becomes an exciting adventure. This book will guide you through the process of embracing continuous improvement with practical strategies, real-world examples, and a healthy dose of humor. We'll break down complex concepts into easy-to-understand steps, making the journey as enjoyable as it is enlightening.

One of the key aspects of continuous improvement is the ability to recognize opportunities for growth. This requires a keen eye for detail and a willingness to critically assess your current innovations. It's about being honest with yourself about what's working and what's not. This book will teach you how to conduct thorough evaluations, name strengths and weaknesses, and set realistic improvement goals.

Setting goals is an essential part of the improvement process. Goals give you direction and purpose, helping you stay focused and motivated. We'll delve into how to set practical improvement goals that propel your innovation forward without overwhelming you.

Once you have your goals, it's time to create a roadmap. This involves outlining the steps needed to achieve your goals, defining milestones, and setting timelines. A well-thought-out plan provides a clear path, ensuring you stay on track and make consistent progress. We'll walk you through the process of developing a comprehensive improvement plan that's tailored to your unique needs.

But planning is just the beginning. Implementation is where the rubber meets the road. This book will equip you with the tools and techniques needed to put our plan into action. From gathering feedback to iterating on your ideas, we'll cover the entire spectrum of the improvement process. You'll learn how to effectively and confirm your enhancements, ensuring they deliver the desired results.

One of the biggest challenges in continuous improvement is keeping momentum. It's easy to start strong but lose steam along the way. We'll share strategies for keeping your motivation high, celebrating small wins, and staying committed to the process. By building and sustaining momentum, you'll ensure your innovation keeps moving forward, even when faced with obstacles.

Obstacles are an inevitable part of any improvement journey. But fear not! This  book will arm you with practical solutions for overcoming common challenges. From resource constraints to resistance to change, we'll tackle the hurdles head-on, providing you with the resilience and persistence needed to succeed.

In today's digital age, technology plays a crucial role in innovation. Leveraging modern tools and technologies can significantly enhance your improvement efforts. We'll explore a range of digital solutions that can streamline tasks, improve efficiency, and offer valuable insights. From automation to data analytics, you'll discover how technology can be your ally in the quest for continuous improvement.

A culture of continuous improvement is vital for long-term success. This involves fostering a growth mindset within your team or organization, encouraging collaboration, and promoting a commitment to excellence. We'll discuss building and nurturing such a culture, ensuring everyone is aligned and motivated to contribute to the improvement process.

Effective communication is another critical part. It's essential to clearly articulate your improvement goals, progress, and results to stakeholders. This book will provide tips on communicating effectively and keeping everyone informed and engaged. By sharing your successes and learning from setbacks, you'll create a transparent and supportive environment.

Measuring the impact of your improvements is crucial. Key Performance Indicators (KPIs) help track progress and evaluate the effectiveness of your efforts. We'll guide you through the definition and measurement of KPIs, ensuring you have a clear understanding of what's working and where further improvements are needed. Data-driven decisions will be your secret weapon.

As we journey through this book, we'll revisit inspiring case studies of companies and individuals who have successfully embraced continuous improvement. These real-world examples will illustrate the principles in action, providing valuable insights and inspiration. You'll see how continuous improvement can lead to remarkable success, from tech giants to small startups.

The conclusion of this book will not be the end but rather a new beginning. By the time you finish reading, you'll have a solid foundation and a comprehensive toolkit for continuous improvement. But remember, the real work begins after you close the book. It's about applying what you've learned, staying committed to the process, and never settling for mediocrity.

So, whether you want to enhance an existing innovation or embark on a new project, this book is your guide to achieving excellence. With a blend of practical advice, real-world examples, and a touch of humor, we'll make the journey of continuous improvement enjoyable and rewarding. Embrace the process, stay curious, and prepare in advance for your innovations.

Welcome to the exciting world of continuous improvement. Let's embark on this adventure together, one step at a time. By the end of this journey, you'll improve your innovations and develop a mindset of perpetual growth and excellence. Here's to continuous improvement, relentless momentum, and a future of innovation and success.

Chapter 2: Assessing Your Current Innovations

Evaluating your current innovations is the first crucial step in continuous improvement. Think of it as a health check-up for your projects. You need to  know what's working, what's not, and where there's room for growth. This chapter will guide you through the innovation process with a keen, critical eye.

Start by gathering all the relevant information about your projects. This includes data on performance, user feedback, and other metrics that can provide insights into how well your innovations function. The more comprehensive your data, the better equipped you'll be to make informed decisions.

Next, conduct a thorough analysis of your data. Look for patterns and trends that can  highlight strengths and weaknesses. Are there areas where your innovation consistently excels? Are there recurring issues or pain points? Finding these patterns will help you pinpoint specific areas that need improvement.

In addition to data analysis, seek feedback from users, stakeholders, and team members. Direct feedback can provide valuable perspectives that data alone might miss. Ask open-ended questions to gain a deeper understanding of the better understanding for improvement. Listening to diverse viewpoints will give you a well-rounded assessment.

Now that you've gathered data and feedback, it's time to find the strengths of your innovations. Celebrate these successes! Recognizing what's working well boosts morale and provides a foundation to build. It is essential to acknowledge and use these strengths as you plan your improvements.

Finding weaknesses is essential. Be honest and aim in this assessment. It can be tempting to downplay issues but facing them head-on is essential for growth. Consider what factors contribute to these weaknesses and how they affect the overall success of your innovation. This critical evaluation is the first step toward meaningful improvement.

Set clear, achievable improvement goals once you've found strengths and weaknesses. These goals should be specific and measurable, providing a clear direction for your efforts. For example, if user feedback shows a need for a more intuitive interface, your goal might be to redesign the interface to improve usability by a certain percentage.

To set practical goals, use the SMART criteria: Specific, Measurable, Achievable, Relevant, and Time-bound. Specific goals provide clarity, measurable goals allow you to track progress, achievable goals ensure they're realistic, relevant goals align with your overall objectives, and time-bound goals set a deadline for completion.

With your goals in place, develop a detailed improvement plan. This plan should outline the steps to achieve each goal, define milestones, and set timelines. A structured plan provides a roadmap to follow, ensuring you stay focused and make progress consistent. The next chapter will dive deeper into creating an effective strategy.

Resource allocation is a critical part of your improvement plan. Decide what resources you'll need—time, budget, personnel—and distribute them  accordingly. Be realistic about what you can achieve with the available resources and prioritize tasks that will have the most significant impact on your innovation.

As you implement your improvement plan, gathering feedback and iterating on your efforts is essential. Improvement is not a one-time task but an ongoing process. Regularly check in with your team and users to gather insights and adjust as needed. This iterative approach ensures that your Innovations continue to evolve and improve.

Testing and validation are essential components of the improvement process. Before rolling out changes, conduct thorough testing to ensure they deliver the desired results. Validate your improvements by measuring their impact against your first goals. This data-driven approach ensures that your efforts are effective and sustainable.

A case study can illustrate the power of thorough assessment and targeted improvements. Look at a company that transformed its innovation through careful evaluation and strategic enhancements. This real-world example will provide practical insights and inspiration for your improvement journey.

Imagine a software company that developed a popular app but noticed a decline in user engagement over time. By analyzing data and gathering feedback, they found key issues such as a confusing interface and frequent crashes. They set specific goals to improve the user experience and distributed resources to address these issues.

The company developed a detailed improvement plan outlining steps to redesign the interface and enhance stability. They conducted extensive testing  to ensure the changes were effective and gathered user feedback to confirm the improvements. The result was a significantly improved app that regained user engagement and satisfaction.

This case study highlights the importance of thorough assessment, strategic planning, and iterative improvement. By following these principles, the company resolved existing issues and positioned itself for long-term success. The lessons learned can be applied to any innovation, regardless of industry or scale.

As you embark on your assessment, remember that continuous improvement is a journey. It requires dedication, curiosity, and a willingness to learn from bosses and failures. Embrace the process, stay committed to your goals, and celebrate every step forward. Improvement is a marathon, not a sprint, and each brings you closer to excellence.

By the end of this chapter, you should clearly understand how to evaluate your current innovations, find strengths and weaknesses, and set achievable improvement goals. This foundation will set the stage for the next steps in your improvement journey. Let's continue building on this momentum and advance your innovations.

Chapter 3: Developing an Improvement Plan

Creating a roadmap for improvement is critical in turning your goals into reality. An effective improvement plan provides a clear path, ensuring you stay focused and professional. Ess cons will guide you through developing a structured, actionable improvement plan tailored to your unique needs.

Start by defining the scope of your improvement plan. What specific areas of your innovation are you looking to enhance? Be as outline: Outline the scope clearly, stay focused, and avoid getting overwhelmed by tackling too many regions simultaneously.

Once you've defined the scope, break down your goals into smaller, manageable tasks. Each task should be a step towards achieving your overall goals. This approach makes the process less daunting and allows you to track progress more effectively. Think of it as building a puzzle —each piece is essential, but the combination of all the pieces creates the complete picture.

Define milestones for each task. Milestones are significant checkpoints that show progress toward your goals. They provide a sense of accomplishment and keep you motivated. For example, if your goal is to improve your app's user interface, a milestone might be completing the redesign of a specific feature.

Set realistic timelines for each task and milestone. Timelines provide a sense of urgency and help you stay on track. However, be realistic about what you can achieve within the given time frame. Overly ambitious timelines can lead to burnout and frustration. Balance ambition with practicality to keep steady progress.

Resource allocation is a critical part of your improvement plan. Decide what resources you'll need to achieve your goals – time, budget, personnel – and distribute them accordingly. Be mindful of any constraints and prioritize tasks that will have the most significant impact on your innovation. Effective resource management ensures that you can execute your plan efficiently.

A detailed improvement plan should also include risk management strategies. Find potential risks that could derail the plan and develop contingency plans to address them. This proactive approach helps you stay prepared for any challenges and ensures that you can quickly get back on track.

Communication is vital to the survival of your improvement plan. Clearly communicate the plan to your team and stakeholders, outlining the goals, tasks, milestones, timelines, and resource allocation. Regularly update them on progress and any changes to the plan. Transparent communication fosters collaboration and keeps everyone aligned and motivated.

As you implement your improvement plan, gather feedback regularly. Feedback offers valuable insights into what's working and what's not. Use this information to make necessary adjustments to your plan. Remember, improvement is an iterative process. Regular feedback loops ensure that your plan evolves and adapts to changing circumstances.

Testing and validation are essential components of your improvement plan. Before rolling out changes, conduct thorough testing to ensure they deliver the desired results.  Validate your improvements by measuring their impact against your first goals. This data-driven approach ensures that your efforts are effective and sustainable.

A sample improvement plan can give a practical example of how to apply these principles. Consider a hypothetical innovation project - a new mobile app to help users manage their finances. The project team has found several areas for improvement, including user interface, functionality, and performance.

The team starts by defining the scope of their ambitious plan. They focus on key areas: redesigning the user interface, adding new features, and perfecting performance. They break down the goal into smaller tasks, such as conducting user research, developing prototypes, and performing stress tests.

They define milestones for each task, such as completing user research by the end of the first month, developing prototypes in the second month, and testing new features in the third month. They set realistic timelines for each task and milestone, ensuring they have enough time to execute them effectively.

Resource allocation is a crucial consideration. The team distributes  specific members to each task based on their ability, sets a budget for development and testing, and creates a timeline that balances urgency with practicality. They also find potential risks, such as technical challenges and user adoption issues, and develop contingency plans to address them.

Communication is emphasized throughout the process. The team holds regular meetings to update each other on progress, discuss challenges, and adjust the plan. They also communicate with stakeholders, providing transparent updates on the project's status and any changes to the plan.

As they implement the plan, they gather feedback from users and stakeholders. They use this feedback to iterate on improvements, ensuring that each change  enhances the user experience. Testing and validation are conducted at each stage, measuring the impact of the improvements against the first goals.

By following a structured approach, the team successfully enhanced their mobile app, delivering a better user experience, adding valuable features, and improving performance. This sample improvement plan illustrates the importance of detailed planning, clear communication, and iterative improvement.

As you develop your own improvement plan, remember that flexibility is critical. Be prepared to adapt and adjust your plan as needed. Continuous improvement is dynamic, and your plan should evolve with changing circumstances. Stay committed to your goals, communicate effectively, and embrace feedback to ensure your plan's success.

By the end of this chapter, you should have a comprehensive understanding of how to develop a structured, actionable improvement plan. This foundation will set the stage for the next steps in your improvement journey. Let's continue building on this momentum and advance your innovations.

Chapter 4: Implementing Feedback and Iteration

Gathering feedback and iterating on your improvements is crucial to

continuous improvement. Feedback offers valuable insights into what's working and what needs further enhancement. This chapter will guide you through thoroughly gathering, interpreting, and implementing feedback to refine your innovations.

Start by naming the sources of feedback. These can include users, team members, and even external experts. Each source provides a unique perspective, helping you comprehensively understand your innovation's strengths and weaknesses. Encourage open and honest feedback, creating an environment where people feel comfortable sharing their thoughts.

Use a variety of methods to gather feedback. Surveys, interviews, focus groups, and user testing are all effective ways to collect insights. Each method has its advantages, so choose the ones that best suit your needs. Surveys can reach a large audience, while interviews and focus groups provide deeper, more nuanced insights. User testing allows you to see how people interact with your innovation in real time.

As you gather feedback, organize and analyze the data to find patterns and trends. Look for recurring themes and common pain points. This analysis will help you prioritize the areas that need the most attention. Use qualitative and quantitative data to gain a well-rounded understanding of the feedback.

Interpreting feedback requires a balanced approach. It's important to consider all perspectives, filter out noise, and focus on the most relevant insights. Look for actionable feedback that provides specific suggestions for improvement. Avoid getting bogged down by vague or contradictory comments. Use your judgment to figure out which feedback aligns with your goals and vision.

"Once you've interpreted the feedback, it's time to implement changes." ("Refining Fashion Designs with Client Feedback - LinkedIn") Start with the most critical impacts on user experience or the overall success of your innovation. Develop a plan for addressing these issues, outlining the improvement steps.

Iterate on your improvements by making incremental changes and testing their impact. This iterative process allows you to refine your innovations gradually, ensuring that each change enhances the overall experience. Conduct regular testing to confirm the effectiveness of your improvements and gather added feedback to guide further iterations.

Testing is a vital part of the iteration process. Use various testing methods to evaluate the impact of your changes. A/B, usability, and performance testing can offer valuable insights. Compare the results of different iterations to decide which changes deliver the best outcomes.

Validation is equally essential. Measure the impact of your improvements against your first goals and KPIs. This data-driven approach ensures that your efforts are practical and align with your aims. Use the validation results to make informed decisions about further iterations.

A case study can illustrate the power of feedback and iteration. Consider a tech startup that developed a new productivity app. First user

Feedback highlighted several issues, including a confusing interface and limited functionality. The team gathered detailed input through surveys and user testing, finding specific areas for improvement.

They prioritized the most critical issues and developed a plan to address them. They gradually refined the app by iterating on the design and functionality and conducting regular testing to confirm each change. The result was a significantly improved app that met user needs and exceeded expectations.

This case study proves the importance of gathering, interpreting, and implementing feedback. The startup could continuously enhance its innovation by embracing an iterative approach, delivering a superior user experience. The lessons learned can be applied to any innovation, regardless of industry or scale.

 Remember that patience and persistence are essential as you implement feedback and iterate on your improvements. Continuous improvement is an ongoing process that requires dedication and a willingness to learn from successes and failures. Embrace the journey, stay open to feedback, and commit to making incremental changes that add up over time.

Effective communication is crucial throughout this process. Keep your team and stakeholders informed about your changes and their reasons. Transparent communication fosters collaboration and ensures that everyone is aligned and motivated. Regularly update them on progress and gather their input to guide further iterations.

Celebrate small wins along the way. Recognize and appreciate the progress you're making, no matter how incremental. Celebrating successes boosts morale and motivation, keeping the momentum going. No matter how small, each improvement brings you closer to your goals.

By the end of this chapter, you should clearly understand how to effectively gather, interpret, and implement feedback. This foundation will set the stage for the next steps in your improvement journey. Let's continue building on this momentum and advance your innovations.

Chapter 5: Building and Sustaining Momentum

Momentum is the driving force that propels your innovations forward. It keeps your moving, even when faced with challenges and setbacks. Building and sustaining momentum is crucial for long-term success. This chapter will provide strategies to support progress, avoid stagnation, and keep your innovation journey on track.

Start by setting clear, achievable goals. "Goals provide direction and purpose, helping you stay focused and motivated." Break down your goals into smaller, manageable tasks, and set milestones to track your progress. Each milestone stands for a significant achievement, giving you a sense of accomplishment and keeping the momentum going.

Create a Sets for your tasks and milestones. Use deadlines to create urgency and help ensure that you stay on track. However, be realistic about what you can achieve within the given time. Balance ambition with practicality to keep steady progress.

Celebrate small wins along the way. Recognize and appreciate the progress  you're making, no matter how incremental. Celebrating successes boosts morale and motivation, keeping the momentum going. No matter how small, each improvement brings you closer to your goals.

Stay flexible and adaptable. Continuous improvement is a dynamic process that requires flexibility and a willingness to adapt to changing circumstances. "Be prepared to adjust your plans and strategies as needed." This adaptability ensures you can navigate obstacles and progress, even when facing challenges.

Communication is key to keeping momentum. Keep your team and stakeholders informed about your progress and any plan changes. Update them regularly on your achievements and gather their input to guide further improvements. Transparent communication fosters collaboration and ensures that everyone is aligned and motivated.

Encourage a culture of continuous improvement within your team or organization. Foster a growth mindset, promoting a commitment to excellence and a willingness to learn from successes and failures. Encourage collaboration and knowledge sharing, creating an environment where everyone is motivated to contribute to the improvement process.

Provide regular feedback and recognition to your team. Acknowledge their efforts and celebrate their contributions. Positive reinforcement boosts morale and motivation, keeping the momentum going. Constructive feedback helps them improve and grow, ensuring everyone strives for excellence continuously.

Leverage technology and tools to streamline your processes and improve efficiency. Modern tools can automate tasks, offer valuable insights, and help you effectively manage your improvement efforts. From project management software to data analytics tools, the right technology can significantly enhance your momentum.

Stay focused on your long-term vision. "It's easy to get caught up in the day-to-day tasks and lose sight of the bigger picture." Regularly revisit your goals and vision to stay motivated and focused. Remind yourself of the long-term benefits of continuous improvement and its impact on your innovation.

A real-life example can illustrate the importance of building and sustaining momentum. Consider a small startup that developed an innovative fitness app. They set clear, achievable goals and created a detailed improvement plan. They supported steady progress by breaking down their goals into smaller tasks and setting milestones.

They celebrated small wins along the way, recognizing and appreciating each achievement. This positive reinforcement boosted morale and motivation, keeping the momentum going. They stayed flexible and adaptable, adjusting their plans and strategies to navigate obstacles and challenges.

Effective communication and collaboration were vital to the critical success. They kept their team and stakeholders informed about their progress, gathering input and feedback to guide further improvements. They encouraged a culture of continuous improvement, fostering a growth mindset and promoting a commitment to excellence.

By using technology and tools, they streamlined their processes and improved efficiency. This allowed them to focus on their core innovation efforts and keep steady momentum. Their long-term vision kept them motivated and focused, ensuring they stayed on track and achieved their goals.

This example proves the importance of building and sustaining momentum. By following these strategies, the startup was able to continuously enhance its innovation, deliver a superior user experience, and achieve long-term success. The lessons learned can be applied to any innovation, regardless of industry or scale.

As you build and sustain momentum in your improvement efforts, remember that persistence and dedication are key. Continuous improvement is a journey that requires ongoing effort and a commitment to excellence. Embrace the process, stay focused on your goals, and celebrate every step forward.

By the end of this chapter, you should have a comprehensive understanding of how to build and sustain momentum in your improvement efforts. This foundation will set the stage for the next steps in your journey. Let's continue building on this momentum and take your innovations in advance

Chapter 6: Overcoming Obstacles and Challenges.

Obstacles and challenges are inevitable in any journey of continuous improvement. How you respond to these challenges can make all the difference. This chapter will equip you with practical solutions for overcoming common barriers, emphasizing resilience and persistence as critical components of success.

Finding potential obstacles is the first step in overcoming them. Common challenges include resource constraints, technical difficulties, resistance to change, and unforeseen setbacks. By expecting these challenges, you can develop proactive strategies to address them before they become major roadblocks.

Resource constraints, such as limited time, budget, or personnel, are a common challenge in the improvement process. Prioritize your tasks and distribute resources based on their impact and feasibility. Consider seeking added resources or finding creative solutions to maximize what you have. Effective resource management ensures you can continue progressing, even with limited resources.

Technical difficulties can derail your improvement efforts. Stay proactive by regularly updating your tools and technologies, conducting thorough testing, and seeking expert advice. Embrace a problem-solving mindset, viewing technical challenges as opportunities to learn and grow. Persistence and creativity are essential to overcoming technical obstacles.

Resistance to change is another common challenge. People are often comfortable with the status quo and may hesitate to embrace new ideas. Communicate the benefits of the proposed changes clearly and involve stakeholders in the improvement process. Address their concerns and provide support to help them adapt. Building a culture of continuous improvement encourages openness to change.

Unforeseen setbacks are a natural part of any improvement journey. Stay flexible and adaptable, prepared to adjust your plans as needed. Maintain a positive attitude and focus on finding solutions rather than dwelling on the setbacks. Resilience and persistence will help you navigate these challenges and keep moving forward.

Problem-solving techniques can help you tackle obstacles effectively. Break the problem into smaller parts, find the root cause, and develop potential solutions. Evaluate the pros and cons of each solution and implement the most possible one. Regularly review and adjust your approach as needed. A systematic problem-solving approach ensures that you can address challenges efficiently.

A case study can illustrate the importance of resilience and persistence in overcoming obstacles. Consider a tech company that faced significant challenges in developing a new software product. They met resource constraints, technical difficulties, and resistance to change within the team.

Despite the limitations, they continued prog to dress by prioritizing tasks and distributing resources effectively. They embraced a problem-solving mindset, viewing technical difficulties as opportunities to innovate. By involving stakeholders and communicating the benefits of the changes, they gradually overcame resistance to change.

Their persistence and resilience paid off. They successfully developed the software product, which became a significant success. This case study proves the importance of finding potential obstacles, developing proactive strategies, and keeping a positive attitude in facing challenges. The lessons learned can be applied to any innovation, regardless of industry or scale.

Remember that resilience and persistence are essential to overcome obstacles in your improvement efforts. Significant challenges are a natural part of the improvement journey, and how you respond to them figures out your success. Embrace a problem-solving mindset, stay flexible and adaptable, and focus on finding solutions.

Effective communication is crucial in overcoming obstacles. Keep your team, and stakeholders informed about your challenges and the steps you take to address them. Transparent communication fosters collaboration and ensures that everyone is aligned and motivated. Regularly update them on progress and gather their input to guide further improvements.

Celebrate your successes, no matter how small. Recognize and appreciate your progress, even in the face of challenges. Celebrating successes boosts morale and motivation, keeping the momentum going. No matter how small, each improvement brings you closer to your goals.

By the end of this chapter, you should comprehensively understand how to overcome common obstacles and challenges in your improvement efforts. This foundation

This will set the stage for the next steps in your journey. Let's continue building on this momentum and advancing your innovations.

Chapter 7: Using Technology and Tools

Technology and tools are crucial for continuous improvement in today's digital  age. Leveraging modern tools can significantly enhance your innovation efforts, streamline tasks, and offer valuable insights. This chapter will explore a range of technologies and tools that can aid in your improvement journey.

Start by naming the specific needs of your improvement efforts. What tasks can be automated? Where do you need more data or insights? What areas could receive help from better collaboration tools? You can do this by understanding the right technologies and tools to support your goals.

Understanding your needs is a powerful way to streamline repetitive tasks and improve efficiency. Look for opportunities to automate data collection, analysis, reporting, and communication processes. Automation tools can save time, reduce errors, and free up resources for more strategic tasks. Embrace automation to enhance your productivity and focus on high-impact activities.

Data analytics tools offer valuable insights into your innovation efforts. Use these tools to collect and analyze data on performance, user behavior, and behaviors. Data-driven decisions are more informed and effective, helping you name improvement areas and measure your efforts' impact. Invest in data analytics tools to gain a deeper understanding of your innovations.

Collaboration tools ease communication and coordination among team members and stakeholders. Project management software, messaging apps, and shared document platforms can enhance collaboration, ensuring everyone is aligned and working towards common goals. Choose collaboration tools that suit your team's needs and preferences to improve efficiency and effectiveness.

A case study can illustrate the power of leveraging technology to improve. Consider a manufacturing company implementing various digital solutions to enhance its production process. They used automation tools to streamline tasks such as inventory management and quality control, significantly improving efficiency and reducing errors.

They invested in data analytics tools to gain insights into production performance and name areas for improvement. They could make informed decisions and improve their processes by analyzing data on production times, defect rates, and machine use. Collaboration tools improved communication and coordination among team members, ensuring everyone was aligned and focused on achieving their goals.

The result was a more efficient and effective production process, with  higher-quality products and reduced costs. This case study proves the importance of leveraging technology and tools for continuous improvement. The lessons learned can be applied to any innovation, regardless of industry or scale.

As you explore the use of tools in your own imprint efforts, remember that the right tools can make a significant difference. Choose tools that align with your needs and goals and invest in training to ensure your team can use them effectively. Stay updated on the latest technological advancements and be open to experimenting with new tools and approaches.

Effective communication is crucial when implementing new technologies and tools. Keep your team and stakeholders informed about the tools you're using, their benefits, and how they support your improvement goals. Provide training and support to ensure everyone is comfortable and proficient with the new tools. Regularly gather feedback and adjust as needed.

Celebrate technology's impact on your improvement efforts. Recognize and appreciate the enhancements that tools and technologies bring to your processes. Celebrating successes boosts morale and motivation, keeping the momentum going. No matter how small, each improvement brings you closer to your goals.

By the end of this chapter, you should have a comprehensive understanding of how to use technology and tools in your improvement efforts. This foundation will set the stage for the next steps in your journey. Let's continue building on this momentum and advance your innovations.

Chapter 8: Building a Culture of Continuous Improvement

A culture of continuous improvement is essential for long-term success. It fosters a growth mindset, encourages collaboration, and promotes a commitment to excellence. This chapter will guide you through building and nurturing a culture of continuous improvement within your team or organization.

Start by fostering a growth mindset. "Encourage your team to view challenges as opportunities for growth and learning." Promote the idea that abilities and intelligence can be developed through dedication and hard work. Create an intelligent mindset that can develop intelligence, create a positive and resilient attitude towards improvement, and foster a continuous learning and development culture.

Promote collaboration and knowledge sharing. Create an environment where team members feel comfortable sharing their ideas, feedback, and experiences. Encourage communication and collaboration, ensuring everyone has a voice in the improvement process. Collaboration fosters innovation and ensures that diverse perspectives are considered.

Invest in training and development to enhance skills and capabilities. Provide opportunities for your team to learn new knowledge and stay updated on the latest industry trends. Training and development are critical components of a culture of continuous improvement, ensuring that your team has the tools and knowledge needed to excel.

Recognize and reward contributions to the improvement process. Celebrate successes and acknowledge the efforts of team members who contribute to your improvement goals. Positive reinforcement boosts morale and motivation, encouraging continued participation in the improvement process. Recognition and rewards create a positive feedback loop, reinforcing a culture of continuous improvement.

Lead by example. As a leader, prove your commitment to continuous improvement through your actions and attitudes. Be open to feedback, embrace challenges, and show a willingness to learn and grow. Your behavior sets the tone for the rest of the team, influencing their attitudes and actions.

A case study can illustrate the  importance of building a culture of continuous improvement. Consider a company that successfully fostered such a culture within its organization. The company promoted a growth mindset, encouraging employees to view challenges as opportunities for growth. It also invested in training and development, ensuring employees had the skills and knowledge needed to excel.

They promoted collaboration and knowledge sharing, creating an environment where employees felt comfortable sharing their ideas and feedback. They recognized and rewarded contributions to the improvement process, boosting morale and motivation. The result was a highly engaged and motivated team that continuously strives for excellence and achieves tangible success.

This case study shows the importance of fostering a growth mindset, promoting collaboration, investing in training and development, recognizing contributions, and leading by example. The lessons learned can be applied to any organization, regardless of industry or scale.

As you build a culture of continuous improvement within your team or organization, remember that it requires ongoing effort and commitment. Foster a growth mindset, promote collaboration, invest in training and development, recognize contributions, and lead by example. Embrace the journey, stay committed to your goals, and celebrate every step forward.

Effective communication is crucial in building a culture of continuous improvement. Keep your team and stakeholders informed about your improvement goals, progress, and achievements. Update their regular plans and gather their input to guide further improvements. Transparent communication fosters collaboration and ensures that everyone is aligned and motivated.

Celebrate your successes, no matter how small. Recognize and appreciate your progress, even in the face of challenges. Celebrating successes boosts morale and motivation, keeping the momentum going. No matter how small, each improvement brings you closer to your goals.

By the end of this chapter, you should comprehensively understand how to build and nurture a culture of continuous improvement within your team or organization. This foundation will set the stage for the next steps in your journey. Let's continue building on this momentum and advance your innovations.

Chapter 9: Measuring and Communicating Results

Measuring the impact of your improvements and effectively communicating the results is crucial for

the success of your continuous improvement efforts. Key Performance Indicators (KPIs) help track progress and evaluate the effectiveness of your efforts. This chapter will guide you through the process of defining and measuring KPIs and ensuring effective communication of your results to stakeholders.

Start by finding the key metrics that align with your improvement goals. These metrics should show progress and success. Examples of KPIs include customer satisfaction scores, defect rates, production times, and financial performance. Choose metrics that are relevant to your specific innovation and goals.

Once you've found the key metrics, set targets for each KPI. "These targets should be specific, measurable, achievable, relevant, and time-bound (SMART)." Clear targets provide a benchmark for measuring progress and evaluating the effectiveness of your improvement efforts.

Collect data regularly to track your KPIs. Use data collection tools and methods that provide correct and reliable information. Regular data collection ensures that you can check progress in real-time and make informed decisions about further improvements. Consistent data collection is crucial for effective measurement.

Analyze the data to gain insights into your progress. Look for patterns and  trends that highlight areas of success and opportunities for improvement. Use qualitative and quantitative data to gain a well-rounded understanding of your performance. Data analysis offers valuable insights that guide your decision-making.

Effective communication of your results is essential. Keep your team and stakeholders informed about your progress and achievements. Share your results using clear and concise reports, presentations, and dashboards. Highlight key successes and areas for further improvement, providing a transparent and comprehensive view of your progress.

Adjust your strategies based on the results. Use the insights gained from data analysis to refine your improvement efforts. Focus on areas that need further enhancement and celebrate the successes. Continuous improvement is an iterative process that requires ongoing adjustments and refinements. Use data-driven decisions to guide your efforts.

A case study can illustrate the importance of measuring and communicating results. Consider a company that implemented a comprehensive KPI tracking system to check their improvement efforts. They found key metrics such as customer satisfaction scores, production times, and defect rates.

They set clear targets for each KPI and collected data regularly to track their progress. They used data analysis tools to gain insights into their performance, naming areas of success and opportunities for improvement. They communicated their results through clear and concise reports, keeping their team and stakeholders informed.

The result was a highly effective improvement process that delivered significant benefits. They were able to make informed decisions, refine their strategies, and achieve their improvement goals. This  case study proves the importance of defining and measuring KPIs, analyzing data, and effectively communicating results. The lessons learned can be applied to any innovation, regardless of industry or scale.

When measuring and communicating your results, remember that consistency and transparency are key. Regularly collect and analyze data, keep your team and stakeholders informed, and adjust your strategies based on the insights gained. Effective measurement and communication ensure that your improvement efforts are successful and sustainable.

Celebrate your successes, no matter how small. Recognize and appreciate your progress, even in the face of challenges. Celebrating successes boosts morale and motivation, keeping the momentum going. Each improvement, no matter how small, brings you closer to your goals.

By the end of this chapter, you should have a comprehensive understanding of how to define and measure KPIs, analyze  data, and effectively communicate your results. This foundation will set the stage for the next steps in your journey. Let's continue building on this momentum and advance your innovations.

Chapter 10: The Power of Persistent Improvement

As we reach the conclusion of our journey together, it's time to reflect on the power of persistent improvement.  Continuous improvement is not just a process; it's a mindset, a way of approaching your innovations with a relentless drive for excellence. This chapter will recap the key lessons learned and provide an inspiring call to action for your future endeavors.

Throughout this book, we've explored the importance of continuous improvement and how it drives long-term success. Each  chapter has provided valuable insights and practical strategies for enhancing your innovations, from assessing your current innovations to developing detailed improvement plans, gathering feedback, and using technology.

One key takeaway is the importance of setting clear, achievable goals. "Goals provide direction and purpose, helping you stay focused and motivated." By breaking down your goals into smaller tasks and setting milestones, you can keep steady progress and celebrate small wins along the way.

Feedback and iteration are critical components of the improvement process. Gathering feedback from users, stakeholders, and team members offers valuable insights into what's working and what needs further enhancement. Iterating on your improvements ensures that each change enhances the overall experience.

Building and sustaining momentum is crucial for long-term success. By setting deadlines, celebrating small wins, staying flexible and adaptable, and promoting a culture of continuous improvement, you can keep the momentum going and achieve remarkable results. Persistence and resilience are key to overcoming obstacles and challenges.

Leveraging technology and tools can significantly enhance your improvement efforts. Automation, data analytics, and collaboration tools provide valuable support, streamlining tasks, and providing insights. Investing in the right tools and technologies ensures that your improvement efforts are effective and efficient.

 A culture of continuous improvement is vital for long-term success. Fostering a growth mindset, promoting collaboration, investing in training and development, recognizing contributions, and leading by example create an environment where everyone is motivated to contribute to the improvement process.

Measuring the impact of your improvements and effectively communicating the results is essential. Defining and tracking KPIs, analyzing data, and sharing your results with stakeholders ensure that your efforts are successful and sustainable. Data-driven decisions guide your improvement efforts and help you achieve your goals.

As we conclude, it's important to recognize that continuous improvement is a journey, not a destination. It requires ongoing effort, dedication, and a commitment to excellence. Embrace the process, stay curious, and never settle for mediocrity. Each step forward brings you closer to your goals and unlocks new levels of success and fulfillment.

Future vision is a crucial aspect of continuous improvement. Envision the long-term benefits of your efforts and stay motivated by the impact you can achieve. Continuous improvement is about building a better future, not just for your innovations but for yourself, your team, and your organization. Keep your vision in mind and let it guide your efforts.

An inspiring call to action: Start improving your innovations today. Don't wait for the perfect moment or the ideal circumstances. The best time to start is now. Apply the principles and strategies outlined in this book to your own projects. Stay committed to the process, celebrate your successes, and learn from your setbacks.

Continuous improvement is a powerful tool for achieving long-term success. By embracing a mindset of persistent improvement, you can unlock new levels of  innovation, efficiency, and impact. The journey may be challenging, but the rewards are well worth the effort. Here's to a future filled with continuous growth and excellence.

As we close this chapter, remember that the journey of continuous improvement is never truly over. Each step forward opens new opportunities for growth and enhancement. Stay committed to your goals, embrace the process, and keep striving for excellence. We can achieve remarkable success and build a future filled with innovation and impact.

Thank you for joining me on this journey. Let's continue building on this momentum and advance your innovations. Here's to the power of persistent improvement and a future filled with success and fulfillment. Cheers to your journey of continuous improvement!

Chapter 11: Practical Solutions for Ongoing Improvement

Continuous improvement requires practical solutions that can be consistently applied over time. This chapter provides a roadmap for readers to  follow in their projects, including practical steps and strategies for ongoing improvement. Maintaining motivation and staying focused on long-term goals are also crucial components of this chapter.

Start by setting up a routine for continuous improvement. Consistency is key to making ongoing progress. Set aside regular time for evaluation, planning, and implementation. Whether it's a weekly review meeting or a monthly check-in, a routine ensures that continuous improvement stays a priority.

Focus on incremental improvements. Small, consistent changes can add up to significant progress over time. Break down larger goals into smaller tasks and tackle them one step at a time. This approach makes the process more manageable and allows you to track progress more effectively.

Use the Plan-Do-Check-Act (PDCA) cycle as a framework for continuous improvement. The PDCA cycle involves planning improvements, implementing them, checking the results, and acting on the findings. This iterative approach ensures that you are continuously evaluating and refining your efforts.

Involve your team in the improvement process. Collaboration and diverse perspectives enhance the quality of your improvements. Encourage team members to share their ideas and feedback and create an environment where everyone feels valued and motivated to contribute. Team involvement fosters innovation and ensures that improvements are comprehensive and effective.

Keep an improvement log to track your progress. Document the changes you've made, the results achieved, and any lessons learned. An improvement log provides a historical record of your efforts, helping you name patterns and make informed decisions about future improvements.

Regularly revisit and revise your improvement goals. As you achieve your goals, set new ones to ensure continuous progress. Revisiting your goals also allows you to adjust them based on changing circumstances and new insights. This dynamic approach keeps your improvement efforts aligned with your long-term vision.

Stay informed about industry trends and best practices. Continuous improvement requires staying updated on your field's latest developments and innovations. Attend conferences, read industry publications, and take part in professional networks to gain new insights and ideas. Staying informed ensures that your improvement efforts are relevant and cutting-edge.

Maintain a positive attitude towards improvement. Embrace challenges and view them as opportunities for growth. "Celebrate successes, no matter how small,  and use setbacks as learning experiences." A positive attitude fosters resilience and persistence, essential qualities for ongoing improvement.

"Invest in training and development for yourself and your team." Continuous learning enhances skills and knowledge, providing the tools needed for effective improvement. Offer opportunities for professional development, such as workshops, courses, and mentorship programs. Investing in training ensures that your team is equipped to drive ongoing improvement.

Use technology to support your improvement efforts. Leverage tools such as project management software, data analytics platforms, and collaboration apps to enhance efficiency and effectiveness. Technology can streamline tasks, offer valuable insights, and ease communication, making your improvement efforts more impactful.

Effective communication is crucial for ongoing improvement. Keep your team and stakeholders informed about your progress, achievements, and future plans. Update them regularly on your efforts and gather their input to guide further improvements. Transparent communication fosters collaboration and ensures that everyone is aligned and motivated.

Maintain motivation by celebrating small wins and recognizing progress. Recognize and appreciate your team's efforts, and celebrate each milestone achieved. Positive reinforcement boosts morale and keeps the momentum going. Celebrating successes creates a positive feedback loop, encouraging continued participation in the improvement process.

Set aside time for reflection and self-assessment. Regularly evaluate your own performance and name areas for personal improvement. Reflecting on your actions and decisions offers valuable insights and helps you grow as a leader. Self-assessment ensures that you are continuously improving your own skills and capabilities.

Encourage a culture of feedback within your team. Create an environment where feedback is welcomed and valued. Encourage team members to share their thoughts and suggestions and use feedback to guide your improvement efforts. A culture of feedback fosters continuous learning and ensures that improvements are comprehensive and effective.

Stay flexible and adaptable. Continuous improvement requires the ability to adjust your plans and strategies as needed. Be open to innovative ideas and approaches and be willing to pivot when necessary. Flexibility ensures that  you can navigate challenges and seize opportunities, keeping your improvement efforts dynamic and relevant.

Measure the impact of your improvements regularly. Use KPIs and other metrics to track your progress and evaluate the effectiveness of your efforts. Regular measurement offers valuable insights and ensures that your improvements are delivering the desired results. Data-driven decisions guide your ongoing improvement efforts.

Celebrate the impact of your improvements. Recognize and appreciate the positive changes that result from your efforts. Celebrating the impact boosts morale and motivation, keeping the momentum going. Each improvement, no matter how small, brings you closer to your long-term goals.

Stay committed to your long-term vision. Continuous improvement is a journey; staying focused on the bigger picture is essential. Regularly revisit your vision and goals to stay motivated and aligned. Your long-term vision provides direction and purpose, guiding your ongoing improvement efforts.

Provide support and resources for your team. Ensure that your team has the tools, training, and support needed to drive continuous improvement. Address any challenges or obstacles they may face and provide guidance and encouragement. Supporting your team ensures that they are motivated and equipped to contribute to the improvement process.

By the end of this chapter, you should have a comprehensive understanding of practical solutions for ongoing improvement. This foundation will set the stage for the next steps in your journey. Let's continue building on this momentum and advance your innovations.

Chapter 12: Keeping Motivation and Commitment to Excellence

Maintaining motivation and staying committed to excellence are crucial  components of the continuous improvement process. This chapter will provide tips for staying motivated and focused on long-term goals, ensuring that your improvement efforts are sustained and impactful.

Start by setting a clear vision for your improvement efforts. Your vision should provide a compelling picture of the future and inspire you and your team to strive for excellence. Regularly revisit your vision to stay motivated and focused on your long-term goals.

Break down your goals into smaller, manageable tasks. Large goals can be overwhelming but breaking them down into smaller tasks makes the process more manageable. Each task completed is a step towards achieving your larger goals, keeping you motivated and making progress more tangible.

Celebrate small wins along the way. Recognize and appreciate the progress you're making, no matter how incremental. Celebrating successes boosts morale and motivation, keeping the momentum going. Each improvement, no matter how small, brings you closer to your goals.

Stay flexible and adaptable. Continuous improvement is a dynamic process that  requires flexibility and a willingness to adapt to changing circumstances. "Be prepared to adjust your plans and strategies as needed." This adaptability ensures that you can navigate obstacles and continue making progress, even in the face of challenges.

Effective communication is key to keeping motivation. Keep your team and stakeholders informed about your progress and any changes to your plans. Update them regularly on your achievements and gather their input to guide further improvements. Transparent communication fosters collaboration and ensures that everyone is aligned and motivated.

Encourage a culture of continuous improvement within your team or organization. Foster a growth mindset, promoting a commitment to excellence and a willingness to learn from both successes and failures. Encourage collaboration and knowledge sharing, creating an environment where everyone is motivated to contribute to the improvement process.

Provide regular feedback and recognition to your team. Acknowledge  their efforts and celebrate their contributions. Positive reinforcement boosts morale and motivation, keeping the momentum going. Constructive feedback helps them improve and grow, ensuring everyone continuously strives for excellence.

Leverage technology and tools to streamline your processes and improve efficiency. Modern tools can automate tasks, offer valuable insights, and help you effectively manage your improvement efforts. From project management software to data analytics tools, the right technology can significantly enhance your momentum.

Stay focused on your long-term vision. "It's easy to get caught up in the day-to-day tasks and lose sight of the bigger picture." Regularly revisit your goals and vision to stay motivated and focused. Remind yourself of the long-term benefits of continuous improvement and its impact on your innovation.

A real-life example can illustrate the importance of building and sustaining momentum. Consider a small startup that developed an innovative fitness app. They set clear, achievable goals and created a detailed improvement plan. They kept steady progress by breaking down their goals into smaller tasks and setting milestones.

They celebrated small wins along the way, recognizing and appreciating each achievement. This positive reinforcement boosted morale and motivation, keeping the momentum going. They stayed flexible and adaptable, adjusting their plans and strategies as needed to navigate obstacles and challenges.

Effective communication and collaboration were key to their success. They kept their team and stakeholders informed about their progress, gathering input and feedback to guide further improvements. They encouraged a culture of continuous improvement, fostering a growth mindset and promoting a commitment to excellence.

By using technology and tools, they streamlined their processes and improved efficiency. This allowed them to focus on their core innovation efforts and support steady momentum. Their long-term vision kept them motivated and focused, ensuring that they stayed on track and achieved their goals.

This example proves the importance of building and sustaining momentum. By following these strategies, the startup was able to continuously enhance its innovation, deliver a superior user experience, and achieve long-term success. The lessons learned can be applied to any innovation, regardless of industry or scale.

As you build and sustain momentum in your improvement efforts, remember that persistence and dedication are key. Continuous improvement is a journey that requires ongoing effort and a commitment to excellence. Embrace the process, stay focused on your goals, and celebrate every step forward.

By the end of this chapter, you should have a comprehensive understanding of how to build and sustain momentum in your improvement efforts. This foundation will set the stage for the next steps in your journey. Let's continue building on this momentum and take your in advance your innovations continuous improvement is a journey, not a destination. Embrace the process, stay committed to your goals, and celebrate every step forward. Here's to your success and the exciting journey ahead!

Conclusion – The Power of Persistent Improvement

As we reach the conclusion of our journey together, it's time to reflect on the power of persistent improvement. Continuous improvement is not just a  process; it's a mindset, a way of approaching your innovations with a relentless drive for excellence. This chapter will recap the key lessons learned and provide an inspiring call to action for your future endeavors.

Throughout this book, we've explored the importance of continuous improvement and how it drives long-term success. Each chapter has provided valuable insights and practical strategies for enhancing your innovations, from assessing your current innovations to developing detailed improvement plans, gathering feedback, and using technology.

One key takeaway is the importance of setting clear, achievable goals. "Goals provide direction and purpose, helping you stay focused and motivated." By breaking down your goals into smaller tasks and setting milestones, you can keep steady progress and celebrate small wins along the way.

Feedback and iteration are critical components of the improvement process. Gathering feedback from users, stakeholders, and team members offers valuable insights into what's working and what needs further enhancement. Iterating on your improvements ensures that each change enhances the overall experience.

Building and sustaining momentum is crucial for long-term success. By setting deadlines, celebrating small wins, staying flexible and adaptable, and promoting a culture of continuous improvement, you can keep the momentum going and achieve remarkable results. Persistence and resilience are key to overcoming obstacles and challenges.

Leveraging technology and tools can significantly enhance your improvement efforts. Automation, data analytics, and collaboration tools provide valuable support, streamlining tasks, and providing insights. Investing in the right tools and technologies ensures that your improvement efforts are effective and efficient.

A culture of continuous improvement is vital for long-term success. Fostering a growth mindset, promoting collaboration, investing in training and development, recognizing contributions, and leading by example create an environment where everyone is motivated to contribute to the improvement process.

Measuring the impact of your improvements and effectively communicating the results is essential. Defining and tracking KPIs, analyzing data, and sharing your results with stakeholders ensure that your efforts are successful and sustainable. Data-driven decisions guide your improvement efforts and help you achieve your goals.

 As we conclude, it's important to recognize that continuous improvement is a journey, not a destination. It requires ongoing effort, dedication, and a commitment to excellence. Embrace the process, stay curious, and never settle for mediocrity. Each step forward brings you closer to your goals and unlocks new levels of success and fulfillment.

Future vision is a crucial aspect of continuous improvement. Envision the long-term benefits of your efforts and stay motivated by the impact you can achieve.  Continuous improvement is about building a better future, not just for your innovations but for yourself, your team, and your organization. Keep your vision in mind and let it guide your efforts.

An inspiring call to action: Start improving your innovations today. Don't wait for the perfect moment or the ideal circumstances. The best time to start is now. Apply the principles and strategies outlined in this book to your own projects. Stay committed to the process, celebrate your successes, and learn from your setbacks.

Continuous improvement is a powerful tool for achieving long-term success. By embracing a mindset of persistent  improvement, you can unlock new levels of innovation, efficiency, and impact. The journey may be challenging, but the rewards are well worth the effort. Here's to a future filled with continuous growth and excellence.

As we close this chapter, remember that the journey of continuous improvement is never truly over. Each step forward opens new opportunities for growth and enhancement. Stay committed to your goals, embrace the process, and keep striving for excellence. We can achieve remarkable success and build a future filled with innovation and impact.

Thank you for joining me on this journey. Let's continue building on this momentum and advance your innovations. Here's to the power of persistent improvement and a future filled with success and fulfillment. Cheers to your journey of continuous improvement!

In closing, it's important to remember that improvement is a continuous process that requires dedication, effort, and a commitment to excellence. By embracing the principles and strategies outlined in this book, you can transform your innovations and achieve long-term success. Stay motivated, stay focused, and keep striving for excellence.

This book has provided you with a comprehensive guide to continuous improvement, offering practical strategies, real-world examples, and a touch of humor to make the journey enjoyable. Whether you're enhancing an existing innovation or embarking on a new project, the principles and strategies outlined here will help you achieve your goals.

As you move forward, remember to celebrate your successes and learn from your setbacks. Each step forward brings you closer to your goals and unlocks new opportunities for growth and improvement. Stay committed to the process, embrace the journey, and keep striving for excellence.

Thank you for embarking on this journey with me. Here's to your success and the exciting journey of continuous improvement ahead. Cheers to the power of persistent improvement and a future filled with innovation and impact. Let's continue building on this momentum and advance your innovations.

In conclusion, continuous improvement is a journey that requires dedication, effort, and a commitment to excellence. By embracing the principles and strategies outlined in this book, you can transform your innovations and achieve long-term success. Stay motivated, stay focused, and keep striving for excellence.

Thank you for joining me on this journey. Here's to the power of persistent improvement and a future filled with success and fulfillment. Let's continue building on this momentum and advance your innovations. Cheers to your journey of continuous improvement!

With this conclusion, we've reached the end of our journey together. I hope you've found the insights and strategies in this book valuable and inspiring. Remember, continuous improvement is a lifelong journey, and the principles you've learned here will serve you well in all your future endeavors.

Stay committed to your goals, embrace the process, and keep striving for excellence. We can achieve remarkable success and build a future filled with innovation and impact. Thank you for joining me on this journey. Here's to your success and the exciting journey of continuous improvement ahead. Cheers!

Check Out A Book Bundle From
Brian's Other Famous Titles
"How To Get Past The Gatekeepers and
Get To Your Goal In Life:
A Personal Guide to Being Persistent"

Bibliography

1. **Covey, Stephen R.** *The 7 Habits of Highly Effective People: Powerful Lessons in Personal Change*. Simon & Schuster, 1989.

2. **Hill, Napoleon.** *Think and Grow Rich*. The Ralston Society, 1937.

3. **Kiyosaki, Robert T.** *Rich Dad Poor Dad: What the Rich Teach Their Kids About Money That the Poor and Middle Class Do Not!*. Plata Publishing, 1997.

4. **Tracy, Brian.** *Goals!: How to Get Everything You Want Faster Than You Ever Thought Possible*. Berrett-Koehler Publishers, 2003.

5. **Sinek, Simon.** *Start with Why: How Great Leaders Inspire Everyone to Take Action*. Portfolio, 2009.

6. **Dweck, Carol S.** *Mindset: The New Psychology of Success*. Ballantine Books, 2006.

7. **Vaynerchuk, Gary.** *Crush It!: Why NOW Is the Time to Cash In on Your Passion*. HarperStudio, 2009.

8. **Cardone, Grant.** *The 10X Rule: The Only Difference Between Success and Failure*. Wiley, 2011.

9. **Ferriss, Timothy.** *The 4-Hour Workweek: Escape 9-5, Live Anywhere, and Join the New Rich*. Crown Publishing Group, 2007.

10. **Thiel, Peter.** *Zero to One: Notes on Startups, or How to Build the Future*. Crown Business, 2014.

11. **Collins, Jim.** *Good to Great: Why Some Companies Make the Leap... and Others Don't*. HarperBusiness, 2001.

12. **Schultz, Howard, and Joanne Gordon.** *Onward: How Starbucks Fought for Its Life without Losing Its Soul*. Rodale Books, 2011.

13. **Maxwell, John C.** *The 21 Irrefutable Laws of Leadership: Follow Them and People Will Follow You*. Thomas Nelson, 1998.

14. **Sincero, Jen.** *You Are a Badass at Making Money: Master the Mindset of Wealth*. Viking, 2017.

15. **Dalio, Ray.** *Principles: Life and Work*. Simon & Schuster, 2017.

NOTES

www.ingramcontent.com/pod-product-compliance
Lightning Source LLC
Chambersburg PA
CBHW071931210526
45479CB00002B/640